# BREAK THE HABIT OF NEGATIVE THOUGHT ADDICTION

FREE YOURSELF FROM HEAD TRASH

SAM J. SHELLEY
LORI PANTAZIS

## CONTENTS

Foreword — vii

1. Life's Adventures — 1
2. Becoming Aware — 19
3. The Quest for Inner Peace — 25
4. Eureka! — 31
5. I Am Not the Exception — 39
6. Mind Full VS. Mindful — 43
7. Perfect Spirit — 47
8. The Iceberg — 49
9. Head Trash — 53
10. Dangerous Habits — 57
11. Daily Mental Shower — 63
12. Recycling the Head Trash — 67
13. Never Criticize Yourself — 71
14. Our Vibration, Our Energy — 73
15. The Head Trash Epidemic — 75
16. Head Trash Anonymous — 77
17. Our Greatest Addiction — 81

Conclusion — 83
About the Authors — 85
Special Thanks — 89

Copyright © 2019 Lori Pantazis and Sam J Shelley

All rights reserved. No part of this publication may be reproduced, distributed, or transmitted in any form or by any means, including photocopying, recording, or other electronic or mechanical methods, without the prior written permission of the publisher, except in the case of brief quotations embodied in critical reviews and certain other noncommercial uses permitted by copyright law. For permission requests, write to the publisher, addressed "Attention: Permissions Coordinator," at the address below.

Front cover image by DesignART

Special edition cover by Poppet 3

Cartoon by Sarah Steenland

Book design by Deviance Press (deviancepress.com)

First printing edition 2019

www.headtrashanonymous.org

*Lori dedicates this book to her precious one-and-only son, Steven, who is her hero and angel on Earth.*

*Sam dedicates this book to his cousins that departed too soon: Heather, Bob, Charlie, and Lorraine.*

# FOREWORD

This is not a self-help or psychology book. This book is about self-empowerment, self-discovery, and self-acceptance. We don't prescribe to, nor adhere to, any particular format or method.

We outline Sam's journey on how he reversed five incurable diseases. It's also about Lori's journey and how she struggled with a traumatic childhood and family life.

Through our combined experiences, we offer suggestions on releasing negative thoughts which can lead to self-destructive habits, low self-esteem, lack of confidence, escapism, etc.

Our goal is for individuals to free themselves from

Head Trash (the non-supportive beliefs, opinions, and judgments).

# 1

## LIFE'S ADVENTURES

### Sam's Journey

I was run over by a van when I was six years old, which resulted in head trauma, a compound fracture of my left elbow, and a broken left hip. I ended up in the hospital for a year and rehab for another six months. In my early twenties, I was institutionalized twice to prevent me from killing myself. Then in my late thirties, I lost the ability to walk and spent several weeks in the hospital and a month in rehab.

Let's start from the beginning.

When I was six years old, on the last day of first grade and the start of summer break, I heard the familiar sound of the ice cream truck playing the Mister Softee ice cream truck theme. I ran to my mom and begged her for money. After getting the money, I ran out the front door and waited for the ice cream truck to come to me. After getting ice cream, I walked around the ice cream truck to go back home. As I was crossing the street, I heard a noise to my left. A van was speeding down the road, and I remember the driver looking to the left (the ice cream truck would be on his right), and I was in the middle of the road! I couldn't move; I felt frozen in place.

After the accident, I had a few glimpses of consciousness: hearing a siren from the ambulance, being wheeled into the bright lights of the operating room. Later that night I felt like I was being placed back into my body, yet I'd had no idea that my beingness had ever left my body.

I always had a sense of guilt that it was my fault for not moving out of the way. I saw the van, yet I couldn't move. Decades later, I read that children don't develop the mental skills of avoidance until their late teens; this is why school zones are posted at 15 mph. I lived unnecessarily with this guilt for decades.

I remember a few distinct things from the accident.

After my soul returned to my body, I recall looking around and seeing a bright, white light and three angels on each side of me. Due to the bright white light, I only saw silhouettes. These angels were very tall and thin, and they didn't have wings. They removed my tubes and life support. I had a near-death experience, yet at the time I didn't know it.

In the morning, my mom asked me, "Why did you remove your tubes?" She didn't ask herself, "How could this child with all these injuries remove the tubes?" Well, Mom was always right, and therefore it had to have been me.

I finally understood the angels' message after writing my first book, *I Don't Dwell*. I'll share my understanding in a later chapter.

I didn't return to school until fourth grade. I had home schooling plus tutoring.

After my recovery, my parents moved to a new town. It was a culture shock. I was a socially awkward kid that would be probably be classified on the autism spectrum today. I had to repeat fourth grade since I didn't pass a placement test in the new school district. This left me feeling deficient and not good enough for the new school.

I didn't have many friends. I was extremely shy, and my social skills were lacking. I remember being stressed out and sickly and gaining lots of weight. I went from being a skinny kid to being husky.

I didn't enjoy my school years. I had severe social anxiety and was often depressed. I remember days in high school in which I would argue with the whole class over something trivial. My parents didn't know what to do with me, and they never sought out psychiatric help for me. Mom would take me to a medical doctor for the physical symptoms, yet I don't remember anyone suggesting mental help despite my earlier brain injury.

After high school, I went to a technical school and received an associate degree in electronics. I'd fallen in love with electronics during my high school days where I could build some gadget in solitude. Being left alone was my happy place.

After school, I got a decent job and I ended up marrying the first person who showed interest in me. I had never dated in high school, and I only dated one girl when I turned twenty, who later became my wife.

In my early twenties, I fell into a severe depression, and at this time I had debilitating migraines. One day the head pain was awful, and life wasn't going well. I went from a good job at General Electric to unknowingly working for a cult. I was easy pickings for the cult since I had terrible self-esteem and needed a sense of belonging. They promised and delivered great money, yet I had to return the money to pay for required courses. It felt like a weird money laundering scheme. On one hand they were giving me money, and on other hand, they were taking back the money to pay for the courses created by the cult founder.

Within a few months, I attended a large cult event in California. At the event, they were singing "Happy Birthday" to the deceased founder and toasting "hip hip hooray," which I found strange. Also around this time, a major magazine publication featured an article which leveled criticism against the cult and made the public aware of their wrong-doings. There was push back from the leaders of the cult, who gave their organizational staff "black media kits" which contained a bunch of propaganda in order to neutralize the bad publicity. Members of the cult and staff were truly brainwashed.

Shortly after the magazine feature, I quit working for them and left. I had no income, no self-esteem, and terrible migraines. I fell into a very dark, severe depression. I remember writing a note to my wife—"Life is too painful, and difficult"—then putting out a bottle of sleeping pills and a glass of water. Right before I would have taken the pills, I had a moment of clarity and called my wife, who took me to the hospital. The darkness of the suicidal mind is hard to describe. I was solely focused on me and my misery, and I had no concern for my wife's well-being.

I saw a psychologist for help, who referred me to a psychiatrist who prescribed anti-depressants. This initial medicine placed me into mania; I had lots of energy, trouble sleeping, and was losing touch with reality. Then I saw another psychiatrist who diagnosed me with bipolar disorder, a disease characterized by severe mood swings, from depression to mania. I was mostly depressed, but on occasion, I would develop a God-like persona and felt like I was invincible. Or like how I had been in the past, arguing with my high school classmates over something trivial.

I was at my weekly psychiatrist appointment when my doctor told me about a call he'd received from a movie producer looking for people that Brad Pitt could interview for his next movie he was filming in Philadelphia. My doctor asked me if I wanted to participate that upcoming Saturday, and I said yes. A few days later, a group of five or six people met at the doctor's office, and from there we walked over to the Korman Suites. When we arrived at the suites, we were greeted by the producer, Chuck Rovin, and another staff member. He told us that we were at the screening room for the movie *12 Monkeys* and told us that Brad would read movie lines and ask us questions. I remember Brad walking in, holding a set of 3x5 index cards. He said hello and a few remarks that I no longer remember; I simply remember him being a very nice guy, humble. He started to read lines from the movie that were on the index cards and asked how they should be portrayed. I didn't just sit there and answer his questions; I stood up and walked over to Brad and role-played a scene with him. If you know the movie, it's the scene where Brad gives a tour of the psych ward to Bruce Willis, in which Brad had an obsession with his chair. I can still watch this movie and see parts of my old self in this scene and movie. It's surreal to see how I was during that period of my life.

The remainder of my twenties, I was stable, yet at times I felt stressed out and overwhelmed with life. I had a good team of doctors that helped me return to a normal life, and I ended up in the IT (Information Technology) field. I worked as a computer manager for a small company, then as an analyst/data specialist at IT consulting firms. I was still bipolar, dealing with my migraines on occasion, with psoriasis (an autoimmune disease that affects the skin) on a third of my body. Then in my early thirties, the psoriasis traveled into my joints (psoriatic arthritis, which is another autoimmune disease).

Then life suddenly took a dramatic change for the worse.

It was a Friday afternoon at work, and I had the worst migraine of my life. It didn't feel like a typical migraine, and deep within I knew something was seriously wrong.

I called my neurologist and explained my symptoms: severe head pain, seeing an aura in my vision, and pins and needles on the left side of my body (which was a new experience). He said it was probably a migraine, and to take my migraine medicine. After taking the medicine and allowing it to work a bit, I drove home. I have no idea how I made it home, but I did. Later that night, my wife and I were alarmed that my symptoms weren't improving, and I still had a lot of head pain with pins and needle sensations. As a result, I ended up in the Emergency Room, where the doctor checked me for a stroke by ordering a CAT scan, in which the results turned out negative. I called my neurologist again in the morning and he gave me a strong painkiller.

On Monday, I had an appointment with my doctor. When I saw the doctor, the head pain was mostly gone, but I still had some pins and needles sensations, and my walking (gait) was affected. He ordered an MRI.

On Tuesday, I had the MRI and walking was a real challenge.

On Wednesday, I got a call from my doctor, who admitted me to the hospital. The first night in the hospital was horrible. I couldn't sleep, and my mind was racing, wondering what was wrong. Would my life ever be the same?

By Thursday, my whole body had shut down, my left eye was jumping around, I couldn't urinate, and walking was impossible. My bipolar symptoms became worse; I went from being stable to unhinged. I was in a dark mental place, and they called in a psychiatrist to adjust my medication.

After a few weeks in the hospital, I was tested for everything and anything. At the age of 37, I was diagnosed with multiple sclerosis (MS), an autoimmune disease of the brain and spinal column that strips away the myelin sheath around the nerves. It felt like my body was being short-circuited without the insulation around the nerves. After the diagnosis, they shipped me off to a rehab center, where I lived for about a month and learned to adjust to life as a disabled man.

By the age of 40, I had a team of six doctors: a neurologist who specialized in migraines, a neurologist who specialized in MS, a psychiatrist for bipolar disorder, a rheumatologist for the psoriatic arthritis, a dermatologist for the psoriasis, and my internal medicine doctor.

I was taking 13 daily medications and a daily injectable medicine. I was using mobility aides (cane or walker) and a cooling vest. The vest had cooling packs for heat-sensitive conditions such as MS. I needed this vest to function because my body would begin to shut down when the temperature rose above 70 degrees Fahrenheit. At 90 degrees, I didn't go outside because this high temperature created a lot of pain and suffering.

Life was terrible, and it was easy to find folks who agreed with me about the horrors of life. It's true that misery loves company.

Lori's Journey

When I was four years old, I was robbed of my innocence when a family member sexually abused me. This abuse went on for years and plunged me into a world of darkness. This abuse became even darker when my parents became aware of the abuse and they blamed me. I felt dirty and ashamed.

My parents protected this monster, which enabled him to continue his destructive and criminal behavior.

One day, the pervert abused the wrong child, and when her parents found out, they threatened police action. My parents spent almost all of their savings to create a blanket of silence.

I had a reprieve when he left to serve the military. Throughout my life though, his interactions with me were inappropriate and continued to perpetuate the pain.

Our family secret stayed with us and died with us.

I lived in the crime-ridden slums of New York City until I was ten. There were frequent incidents of murders, rape, prostitution, drug trafficking, and gang wars.

I recall one rainy day in the slums when my sister and I were being pursued by a would-be attacker. We frantically ran home, and in our haste, the umbrella broke. My father punished us because of the broken umbrella, despite him knowing that we were being chased. We couldn't understand why we were being punished. This left us anxious and confused. What did we do wrong? We were trying to prevent being beaten, murdered, or raped. This is one example out of many that I experienced that set the stage for future issues with self-worth, self-esteem, self-blame, night terrors, and personal safety.

After living in the slums, we moved into a nicer neighborhood in the borough of Queens. Life improved, yet I felt extremely awkward. I was behind in school because of the prior poor-quality education from my slum school. My peers seemed so much more sophisticated than me. They had larger allowances, better clothes, and they were better educated. I was catapulted into a different world. I felt like a slum dog reject.

Life became more complicated when I reached puberty at age 11. I felt even more ashamed with the major changes in my body. I took my self-hate to a new level. When I reached my early teens, I had men looking at me as if I were a sexual object, and with my history of abuse, this brought up deep-seated feelings of shame and guilt.

I was an unpopular loner throughout middle school and high school. I dropped out of high school six months before I would have graduated. My parents seemed indifferent and offered no guidance. A few months later, I fell into a deep depression and threatened suicide. My mother took me to a psychiatrist who prescribed strong medication for depression. I became a vegetable, sleeping for endless hours and crying all the time.

In my late teens, I started dating. I made poor choices while I was dating, and before I knew it, I was married with a baby. It's not surprising that I picked someone verbally and physically abusive. Eventually, I decided to end this terrible marriage.

The years following my divorce was a difficult uphill climb. Liberation from my heartless husband came with a price. This took place at a time before being a single parent became a common occurrence. I was anxious and feeling guilty, wondering what the psychological impact would be on my young son. I knew that constant exposure to his ignorant father was destructive. For instance, my husband would tell his toddler son that boys don't cry. In another instance, he smacked his three-year-old child for putting his finger on a freshly painted wall. Yet I still felt sad and deeply concerned about my son growing up in a single parent household.

When I started to doubt whether a divorce was the correct course of action, I would think back to certain incidents that were turning points in my unhappy marriage and had led to my decision. A few incidents stood out that were defining moments and had led to separation, then divorce. For a few years when my child was very young, I was a stay at home mom. My husband would give me just enough money to buy groceries with very little pocket money left over. I still managed to save enough money to buy clothes for my son. I recall when my husband returned home that night, and I was all excited and showed him the purchases. I was shocked when he screamed at me and made me return the clothes because I'd failed to ask for his permission before purchasing the clothing. Another upsetting incident occurred one morning when I made my husband soft boiled eggs, which were his favorite. I put a teaspoon down on the table. He then flew into a rage because he'd wanted a tablespoon instead of a teaspoon. He took the eggs and threw them at the wall. I was horrified that my son was witnessing this incident. He stared at the tossed eggs running down the wall. His dad was his hero, his role model. Would my son grow up thinking that it's okay to treat people this way? Would he go on to treat women poorly?

I found out through a trusted source that my husband was living a double life. He had an apartment in Brooklyn, and we lived in Queens. He kept company with a young woman. This would account for the fact that my husband would disappear for weeks at a time, without telling where he was going or when he would come back. In one instance, I ran out of money and had to ask my parents for help. I was humiliated and ashamed.

Once I was 100% certain that I was going through with the divorce, I took the necessary steps to make sure I could support and take care of my child. I proceeded to get my high school equivalency diploma and enroll in college. I also had to find a job. I had few marketable skills but fortunately I had been a waitress, so I looked for restaurant work. I landed a job as a part-time cocktail waitress at a major hotel in Manhattan. Soon after, the job became full time. I made more than adequate income and was able to be self-sufficient, pay all the overhead bills, and still have enough money left over to pay for a babysitter and my college education.

Life was exhausting because I worked overnight into the wee hours of the morning. Then a few hours later, I would go to class while my son was in school. I didn't get to spend a lot of time with my son, except for my days off. As a result, I was verbally attacked and criticized by my family. They felt I should have applied for public assistance and stayed at home with my son. I refused to take this course of action. I wanted to be self-supporting and self-sufficient. I'd grown up poor and had suffered as a result. I didn't have nice clothes, a good allowance, nor was I able to eat out and enjoy my life. I didn't want my son to experience this sense of poverty and lack.

2
---
# BECOMING AWARE

## Sam's World

Besides work, I was mostly a coach potato. I would go to the gym on occasion and try to improve my physical situation. When I did go to the gym, I had to wear my cooling vest and try not to overheat. I usually did overheat, and I would walk out feeling more crippled due to the spasticity (muscle spasms) in my legs, which was a symptom of MS. Then a few hours later, I would end up with a migraine if I'd pushed myself too hard at the gym.

I would watch anything and everything on TV. I found ghost hunting shows fascinating, but I was a skeptic; it was TV and it could be scripted. One day, I saw a tweet from a Ghost Hunter about an event at Fort Mifflin in Philadelphia. I was naturally curious and decided to attend. The skeptic in me wanted to see if ghosts were real.

I did my research on Fort Mifflin and discovered which parts were the most haunted, active areas. I decided that I would head to the casemates (small rooms in a fortress used to hold munitions). During the Civil War, the casemates had been used as a prison for Confederate soldiers.

On the day of the event, I arrived with my cooling vest and my quad cane. I could only attend for an hour or so before the cooling packs in the vest melted.

We were spilt into groups. I joined the group that was going to the casemates. For the first half hour or so, I was bored because not much was happening. Then someone put out a twist flashlight several feet away from them and said "turn this flashlight on," and it went on. Then they said "turn this flashlight off," and it went off. This back and forth went on for several minutes. The skeptic in me said "that's their flashlight," so I put my flashlight out and it did the same thing! I also had on occasion felt a feeling of dread, and once during that night I'd felt like someone had sat down next to me, but I couldn't see them.

This event left me with a lot of questions. I began to read some books to better understand what I'd experienced. My eye sight was extremely poor from the MS, and reading more than a few pages would give me a migraine.

Eventually, I stumbled upon a book that talked about meditation and its benefits. One benefit jumped out at me—inner peace. I desperately needed inner peace since I was frequently in a stressed-out state, wondering what else was going to go wrong.

The book didn't give detailed instructions on how to meditate, just simple instructions to sit some place quiet, play soft background music, and relax. This was a blessing; if you'd told my bipolar, obsessive-compulsive mind that there were rules to meditation, I would have been so focused and fixated on the rules that I would have never cleared my head trash.

I could imagine my brain with formal instructions. *Am I sitting correctly? Am I holding my hands correctly? Am I breathing correctly? Will this music bring inner peace?* And so on...

Lori's World

When I was around fifteen years old, a new world opened up to me. I read my first Edgar Casey book, and it was an introduction to the concept of karma. My life suddenly made sense to me; I felt like I was being punished for being a bad person in this life, and that I must have been a terrible person in a past life (or lives). I took a spiritual concept and turned it into a weapon of blame and self-hatred. I didn't understand that difficult situations were learning experiences, not punishments. The exposure to spiritual concepts, however, was important, and later would serve me well.

Around the same time, I also became fascinated with astronomy. I read everything I could on the subject. My fascination with the stars and heavenly bodies took on a new dimension when I started to study—and later practice—astrology. Learning astrology was an enlightening discovery that a person's karma is reflected in the natal chart, which is the blueprint or DNA of one's life. I was able to build on the knowledge that I'd absorbed from Edgar Casey's work and correlate his concepts of karma with astro analysis. At the very least, my exposure to the spiritual world helped give me hope and helped me cope.

# 3

## THE QUEST FOR INNER PEACE

### Sam's Journey

After reading about how meditation brings inner peace, I sat quietly for five minutes that night and followed the book's suggestions. I had a piece of soft music playing in the background. The music served as my timer, since the music track was about five minutes in length.

The first two weeks of meditation were difficult. Somehow, I gained the impression that meditation meant the mind stopped thinking. Then one day, I had a profound realization: I have thoughts, but I am not my thoughts. Meditation didn't mean you had to stop thinking, it was just a way to know yourself as the witness to your thoughts.

I don't like the term *meditation practice*. I prefer *skilled relaxation*. I've met many angry and upset meditators! The mind is under control when you're in a controlled environment like meditation. When you're going through the experience of life, and the mind doesn't like what's happening, then chaos may ensue. Chaos ensues when the mind is not fully aware of the current moment and is instead dwelling on a mental story.

My practice began with five minutes a day of skilled relaxation. After the first two weeks of struggle, I found my practice. When the mind would get busy thinking about what I needed to do, what had happened earlier in the day, or some other distraction, I would ask myself phrases: *Where are my feet? What do I see? Where are my hands?* This forced the mind into the present moment, and I discovered that when I was lost in the story (mental distractions are the head trash), I wasn't fully there in that moment. My body was there, but my mind was a time traveler.

After a few weeks, I began to sit for five minutes twice a day, and then a month later I would sit for ten minutes twice a day. After this practice, I was gaining inner peace as I learned to keep the mind in the here and now.

My skilled relaxation practice:

- Sit quietly.
- Close the eyes to remove external distractions.
- When they mind gets distracted, bring the mind back by asking questions about your body or environment: *Where are my feet? Where are my hands? What do I hear?*
- As your practice progresses, you will stop asking questions. You will simply notice the body sensations and bring your mind back to this moment.
- Repeat the above process.

When you're unable to bring the mind back to the moment, STOP! Staying with a distracted mind creates stronger mental stories.

Even if you had intended to sit for a prescribed amount of time, don't adhere to this if the mind becomes overly active and restless. Get up and do something else.

## Lori's Journey

As a single mom working full time and going to school to get my bachelor's and then my master's degree, I had little free time. All that changed when I graduated from college. I was a very anxious, nervous, and fidgety person, and I needed clarity and direction, so I decided to learn to meditate. I tried different techniques such as guided meditation, progressive relaxation, and visualization, among others. For me, I found I got the best results by sitting quietly and allowing information to come to me effortlessly. I had snippets of amazing realization, and oftentimes, I experienced deep relaxation that resulted in decisiveness, better concentration, and inner resolve. Sometimes, I felt unconditional love that brought tears to my eyes and overwhelming emotion. I then noticed the remarkable changes that ensued. I realize now that I had such good results because I didn't adhere to a prescribed formula. I just sat still noticing my thoughts, and in time the incessant chatter quieted.

I had a deep new awakening, and the transformation was dramatic. I experienced a new way to view the world, and I felt optimistic. My inner growth was steady and is still continuing.

# 4

## EUREKA!

Sam's Ah-Ha Moment

I had been doing my practice for roughly three months when everything changed. One evening, I was just sitting there after my evening practice and looking around the room, and I heard a gentle, male voice say "Perfect Spirit." Eureka! That's it! I'm a Perfect Spirit; it's the body and mind that are damaged.

After hearing this voice, I simply had a deep knowing that all was well, and then all sense of fear about my health went away.

After hearing the voice, my mind became mostly quiet. After having suffered with the negative voice in my head, I was finally free of my debilitating thoughts. I no longer woke up with the "woe is me" mindset. I woke up in a positive frame of mind, looking forward to the day ahead.

After the mental noise quieted, my intuitive voice became louder. It had always been there whispering to me, but it had always been drowned out due to the screaming, protesting mind.

Have you ever had a hunch that you should do a task a certain way, but then the mind came along and convinced you to do it another way? Then you look back and say to yourself, "I should have done it the first way." The hunch was your intuitive voice, your Wayshower, on the proper direction. One of the hardest things to do is to trust ourselves. Trust comes from a practice of learning to believe our own wisdom, and not allowing the head trash to create confusion and doubts.

I followed this intuitive voice to mend the body and mind.

I'm not a doctor, so don't do this without your doctor's approval; I simply knew it was time to cut back my medications. I had no fear, even though It had taken years to get my medicine correct to live a relatively normal life. Slowly and steadily, I cut my medications back and sixteen months later, I was taking no medication.

I just knew one day that I needed to do yoga. My mind protested and said, "No way, your balance is too poor, you aren't flexible." The mind loves its story based on some fantasy. I had never done yoga before, so why did the mind insist that I couldn't do it? Ignoring the mind, I moved forward and set the intention to do yoga. I looked on the Internet and saw there were many types of practices. I didn't know which form of yoga to do. Then the following day, I was driving to work. About 20 minutes into my drive, I had a knowing that the small yoga studio to my right in a small shopping center was where I needed to be. The intuitive voice will give you one step at a time, which the mind finds difficult since it prefers to know all the details.

---

**Exercise #1: Ignoring the Mind**

Think of a time when your mind expressed a belief or opinion that something wasn't for you, despite you never having had the experience. A situation when the mind was guessing, not basing anything on facts. My mind would frequently do this with foods or exercises.

Another common example is a work opportunity, where the mind will give you a false story that you don't have the skills or talent to perform a job, thus making you pass up a potential opportunity that could have changed your life. As Richard Branson states, when someone offers you an opportunity, just say "Yes!" and figure it out later. Take a moment to reflect on where the mind has derailed you. By becoming aware of these stories and head trash, you begin to take back control of your life.

Writing these mental distortions down in a journal is a good way to remind yourself of the stories. The more aware of the stories you become, the better life will become.

---

When I got to work, I looked up River Yoga and saw their schedule. I made plans to attend the Yin yoga class with RaeAnn (poses are held for two to three minutes, and I enjoyed the stretching). The following Monday, I went to a Vinyasa yoga class with David (very active class, and quite the challenge!). I remember RaeAnn loading me up with props to maintain the poses. I remember the kindness of David helping me out. In the beginning of Vinyasa, my balance was very poor, and I would get tipsy, yet I stuck with it. I would attend three or four yoga classes a week, mostly Vinyasa classes with one Yin class a week. I no longer attended the traditional gym with lifting weights and cardio machines.

Six months later, I didn't need a cane or walker.

Over a period of nineteen months—from the beginning of my skilled relaxation process to complete restoration of my health—I did what I didn't set out to do. I simply wanted inner peace which I accomplished, yet I never considered healing myself of all my diseases.

By clearing my head trash, I created space for transformation.

### Lori's Perspective on Her Eureka! Moment

My healing was gradual and incremental. Most people go through a gradual change, and very few have a big Eureka! moment like Sam (Wayne Dyer called them "quantum shifts").

I often asked myself, "Why am I such a failure?" I started gaining insight when I went for marriage counseling with my ex-husband. My husband was completely uncooperative, and after a short period of time, he ended our therapy. I continued with the therapist for a few months after. Through this, I became aware of just how destructive my marriage was. I spoke about the cruelty, infidelity, and shameful behavior of my husband. The abuse was staring me in the face. Through it all, I still felt it was mostly my fault, and I continued to blame myself for my failed marriage. I felt incredible guilty that we were putting our child through this chaos. At least I recognized that my husband had broken our marital vows and betrayed me. This was the beginning of recognition that my husband was also responsible for our serious marital problems.

Another milestone occurred around this time

when I was an undergraduate student. I took a course called *The Psychology of Communication*. During this course, the students got to understand the system of relating. We learned the psychology of interaction and the roles individuals play. For example, if one person is a teacher, the other person plays the role of a student. In an unhealthy relationship, for instance, one person is the abuser and the other is the victim. A system of relating collapses when a person stops playing his or her designated role, changing their responses to the dominant person. I could see how I had participated in playing the role of a victim. I learned how to stand up for myself, and I noticed the immense changes that occurred. This was a breakthrough for me.

5

# I AM NOT THE EXCEPTION

Sam's Perception

When my first book, *I Don't Dwell,* was released, I had a public relations person reach out to the media to do book interviews. The media wanted feel-good stories, yet my story was too good to be true! I had reversed five "incurable" diseases, which was an "impossible" concept for the general public. When I hear "impossible," I know there is a mental story (head trash) attached that is creating a limitation. Without the head trash creating false limitations, all things are possible.

My doctors couldn't explain my healing. The last time I saw my neurologist, he questioned me for 45 minutes, trying to quantify what I'd done. He wasn't accepting the fact that I'd heard "Perfect Spirit" and followed my intuitive voice on the steps to heal.

I spoke to physician Dr. Gabor Mate at a conference and told him how I'd healed myself. He asked a few questions then said, "Oh, you stopped believing your mind."

I have witnessed many miracles when individuals stopped believing their mind, or you could say they surrendered the mind and instead listened to their own intuitive voice. I worked with someone who went from stage four breast cancer that had metastasized into her bones and organs; she went from facing death to now living a normal life. I also worked with a man who'd had severe social anxiety, who couldn't work, and is now happily employed.

You can search the Internet and find many miracles. I'm willing to guess your mind has a story about how these "miracle makers" must be special in some way. This story is head trash and is blocking your own miracle(s). Miracles are normal when the mind isn't creating interference.

When I was six years old, surrounded by angels

that removed my life support, I didn't understand their purpose at that time. But after healing myself of five incurable diseases, I understood the teachings from the angels: "You don't need the outside influences to heal yourself. You can heal yourself."

Everyone is a limitless Perfect Spirit. The only limitations are coming from the head trash! Clearing the head trash creates the space for transformation!

Lori's Perspective

Sam, and other extraordinary healers, are not extraordinary at all. Everyone can quiet the mind, relax, and allow their Perfect Spirit to guide them through a healing experience. I'm not saying that one should not get medical attention; medical intervention can be lifesaving. I am, however, referring to connecting to your own wisdom and inner guidance. If you are under medical treatment, the healing process may be accelerated by allowing intuitive information to be processed by the conscious mind.

As a teacher and counselor, I've observed positive

changes in others. I've worked with clients who realized through astro analysis where the origins of their potential destructive behavior lie in the natal chart. I've also done energy work on individuals who suffered from an assortment of physical ailments, and I noticed the positive improvements in their physical conditions after just a few sessions. For example, when I was working at a senior center, I helped a lady with severe joint pain who could barely lift her arm. She went from being in debilitating pain to feeling only mild discomfort.

## 6

## MIND FULL VS. MINDFUL

There are two popular cartoons that illustrate mind full vs. mindful perfectly.

In one cartoon, a man is sitting on a park bench with his dog, seemingly enjoying the day. The man has a bubble showing his thoughts, and all his thoughts are from the past and have nothing to do with the current park scene. Meanwhile, the bubble showing the dog's thoughts are merely images of the park.

In the other cartoon, a man is standing next to a horse on a beautiful vista overlooking the desert. The bubble showing the man's thoughts are filled with all sorts of stuff, but nothing of the desert in front of him. Meanwhile, the bubble showing the horse's thought are merely images on the desert.

Both cartoons have a similar caption: paraphrased, "Learn to be present and enjoy the moment."

In the previous chapters, we showed how our life experiences filled our minds with clutter—we call this head trash. The head trash is taking you out of the moment.

In the upcoming chapters, we detail on how to clear out the clutter, which allows you to fully enjoy life—right here, right now—without dragging in the past or guessing about the future.

---

**Exercise #2: Identifying Mind Full VS. Mindful**

Think back to an earlier time when you were at a romantic dinner, on a vacation, or at a social gathering, and you were feeling anxious and distracted. What thoughts did you have in your mind? Were you obsessing over work or a previous past event? How did your body feel? These questions will help you identify being mind full vs. mindful.

---

## 7

## PERFECT SPIRIT

Perhaps the term *Perfect Spirit* still doesn't make sense to you. Grab a bunch of photos of yourself at different ages and notice all your different bodies. If the bodies are changing, then what isn't changing? The one who sees through the eyes—the one who tastes, the one that hears, the one that feels. This is your consciousness, or your Perfect Spirit or life.

Without really knowing yourself as spirit, the mind will continue to believe that you're the mental story. Use the techniques listed in this book to put a dent into the story, and know that the real you is a Perfect Spirit. You are a spiritual being having a human experience.

From a place of Perfect Spirit, all is well. Spirit sees your life as a series of experiences, where all experiences are here to help us learn and grow. Everything happens for our benefit. No experience is good nor bad. The judgment of good or bad comes from the mind, which is basing this on a past experience or future guessing on what this might be like. The mind is a time traveler, rarely aware of the present moment. The mind confuses your life experience with life. Eckhart Tolle calls this confusion "madness."

In the past, Sam only knew himself as a body and a mind; he had no understanding that his true self was a spiritual being. He had heard that he was a spiritual being, but this was not his reality. If he were a spiritual being, why was his body and mind so sick?

## 8

## THE ICEBERG

The mind is like an iceberg, and it has two basic components: the conscious mind and the subconscious mind. We usually aren't aware of the beliefs, opinions, and judgments in the cumulative head trash buried in our subconscious, until the conscious mind fires off a trigger.

For example, you may be doing an affirmation: "I create prosperity easily and effortlessly." If your subconscious learned a belief system from your parents that working hard creates money, then this affirmation is just words that the subconscious easily dismisses. If the conscious mind doesn't match the ingrained belief system that's in the subconscious mind, then the conscious mind will reject the notion.

Remember—uncovering blocks is the first step toward healing. These are pivotal moments in your self-discovery. When you've uncovered blocks, you've struck gold.

Our upbringing and life experiences become ground zero for our BS (belief systems).

To change our beliefs, opinions, and judgments that are locked in the subconscious, we need to approach from the level of Perfect Spirit. Use Perfect Sprit plus the conscious mind to reprogram the subconscious.

If you desire to do this in an affirmation approach, then you would say, "There is one Perfect Spirit, one energy, and I know that I am a part of this Perfect Spirit, one energy." You need to merge into a state of oneness before continuing. At the deepest level, everything is energy within the quantum field (which is the level of transcendence). This lowest level of energy is the zero point, which is neutral. Think of the Universe as a genie—"your wish is my command." What you think about, you bring about.

When you say your affirmation, you need to be in an emotional state of joy or happiness, which is an elevated vibration that provides the energy to create change in the subconscious. "I create prosperity easily and effortlessly. And so, it is."

Don't concern yourself with the details; a mind focused on "how to?"' is a mind that blocks. You turn this over to Perfect Spirit to execute. Perfect Spirit will provide guidance that you need to act upon. When Sam was going through his healing practice, he simply had an intuitive knowing—do yoga, watch less TV, drink more water, eat less meat, etc.—that provided the recipe to recovery of the body and mind. Perfect Spirit will provide the steps that we need to create healing and transformation (inspired action).

Also, the mind doesn't know the difference between reality and imagination/fantasy. For example, someone may be afraid of heights, spiders, people, etc. You can lead them into their imagination and have them experience all their phobias while sitting in the safety of their couch. Close your eyes and imagine a huge spider crawling on your arm, or close your eyes and imagine that you're sitting on the ledge of a very tall building. How does your body respond if you have these phobias?

## 9

### HEAD TRASH

Head trash consists of thoughts that are taking you out of the present moment, which is the here and now.

The head trash is the root cause of stress, poor self-esteem, depression, anxiety, panic attacks, lack of self-love, and a lack—or poverty—mindset. Additional indications are: poor self-image, chronic criticism of self and others, distorted vision of one's being, jealousy, fear, anger, greed, constantly comparing oneself to others, aggressive and perhaps violent behavior, insomnia or excessive sleeping, eating disorders such as anorexia or overeating, escapism, nervousness, restlessness, and addictions. The head trash comes in thousands of forms and flavors. No one is excluded from head trash, because everyone has a mind that thinks!

There are five depths to the head trash, and the older you are, the more you accumulate, unless you develop a clearing practice. From our experience, if you have a lot of early traumas, you pick up head trash earlier and more easily.

The five depths of head trash: none, waste paper basket, trashcan, dumpster, and landfill.

**Note:** Few people on Earth have achieved a state of emptiness. Some call this *Enlightenment*. We define Enlightenment as knowing that all is well, despite the mind's opinion.

**Waste Paper Basket:** A small amount of head trash. Mild manifestations of mental, emotional, and physical discomfort. Experiencing bouts of indecisiveness and moodiness because you don't know why you feel a certain way. You're confused because you know something's wrong, but you don't know what it is.

**Trashcan:** A moderate amount of head trash. Symptoms of distress that are pronounced and interfere with daily functioning.

**Dumpster:** A large amount of head trash. You are consumed with obsessive focus on feeling mentally and physically ill. Nothing is working for you anymore.

**Landfill:** A massive amount of head trash. Serious and perhaps life threatening mental, physical, and emotional diseases.

When Sam had five diseases (three autoimmune diseases), was suicidal, and had PTSD, social anxiety, and panic attacks, he had a landfill of garbage that needed to be removed.

Lori's Perspective

Looking at the five levels of head trash, I can say that I was at the dumpster level. I had the following symptoms: anxiety attacks, feeling like a social outcast (social anxiety), and an obsession about my physical appearance. Growing up in the slums, we were very poor, leaving me with a poverty consciousness.

**Exercise #3: Rate Your Head Trash**

Based on the five depths of the head trash above, where would you rate your head trash? You would need to consider the amount of non-stop thinking, anxiety, and tension and tightness in the body. Are you chronically feeling unhealthy?

Feel free to share your story on the Facebook Head Trash Anonymous Global Chapter, which is listed and described later in the book.

10
---

# DANGEROUS HABITS

Sam's World

I would wake up each day and ask myself, "What else is going to go wrong?" Typically, something would go wrong. I developed a "woe is me" mindset.

I also had no confidence and was extremely self-critical. I felt that I wasn't good enough and that I needed to do better.

My natural curiosity added to my poor mindset, since I would read everything about my ailments and the side effects of the medicine I was taking. I knew so much about my ailments, which filled my mind with fear (my mind would create a future life in a wheelchair!). The worst thing I did was read about side effects of my medicine. This took my stress to new heights! I had a huge list of possibilities on what could go wrong.

My most destructive habit was dwelling in my negative "woe is me" mindset. I was unaware that this dwelling in the negative mindset was creating hell on Earth.

Lori's World

I was completely unaware of how my destructive childhood affected my behavior and self-image. My earliest memory is a distorted view of myself. I always felt different from others. I felt inferior in every way. Even though I did very well academically and received good grades, I still believed I was stupid. This was exacerbated by the fact that I decided to drop out of high school.

I lived in a state of fear and anxiety. I took menial jobs that paid poorly. Every time I was confronted with a new task to learn, I became paralyzed with fear. I aimed low, and I was an underachiever.

My self-image was poor. I considered myself ugly and unappealing in all ways, despite positive input by others. I only paid attention to those who criticized me. I judged myself harshly, and I was my own worst enemy. I was certain that I was damaged goods, and that no one would want me.

Another example of my distorted self-image manifested in my belief that I was overweight, even though my weight was normal. I was constantly dieting, and no matter how thin I got, I still was certain that I was too heavy.

My lack of confidence manifested in many ways. I dated men who were uneducated and not very good-looking. Some of these men had criminal records. One of the young men I dated died of an overdose of drugs. I stopped dating when I married my abusive, mean husband.

I became a people pleaser and said yes instead of saying no when asked to do favors for friends or family members. Sometimes, it was inconvenient to do these favors, but I still did them anyway. I was a doormat in my marriage and with my friends. I never stood up for myself because I felt I didn't deserve to be liked or loved. I was always afraid of offending others, and I kept my opinions to myself.

I didn't value myself and I felt lost, confused, and generally miserable. I was in a state of suspended animation because I was mentally crippled and didn't and couldn't make decisions. I didn't trust my judgment. I blamed myself for anything and everything that went wrong. In addition, I repressed my feelings and held everything in. I numbed myself and didn't let myself express my emotions. I was closed off and I isolated myself. People thought I was cold, indifferent, and selfish. I just couldn't get things right. I lived in a state of dread, helplessness, and hopelessness. I was terrified that others would find out the truth about me and that my secrets buried within would surface. Then they would see how dirty and cheap I was. My shame overshadowed my need to connect with others and have a normal life. I was trapped in a self-made hell. I believed there was something weird and disgusting about me. My self-loathing defined me.

General

Sam asked his Facebook friends what their most dangerous habit was, and here are some of their responses.

"Not caring for myself—defining myself by my caring for others."

"Dwelling on the past and keeping the anger about past situations."

"Getting stuck, feeling paralyzed by fear, and isolating myself because I don't want to bother people who have 'real problems,' or 'more important friends.'"

"I belittle and shame myself. I say 'I cannot' a lot."

"People pleasing and lack of boundaries in intimate relationships."

"Laziness."

---

**Exercise #4**

Take a moment and ask yourself, "What is my most dangerous habit?"

Write this down and a little later you'll learn how to clear this mental garbage (head trash).

---

## 11

## DAILY MENTAL SHOWER

We take a physical shower to wash away the daily dirt, so why aren't we taught to take a daily mental shower to wash away the negative thoughts, beliefs, opinions, and judgments that we picked up throughout the day?

This process requires using our imagination.

Sam's version

- Begin with a skilled relaxation process to quiet the mind for 1-2 minutes.
- After a few minutes of relaxation, imagine a showerhead with a hose above you.
- Flowing out from the showerhead is a gold

energy. It's entering the top of the head, flowing down the spinal column, flowing through the nervous system, down through the legs, and exiting out through the feet.
- Next, bring up any stories (beliefs, opinions, judgment, or emotions) that came up for you today. You can even do this for past pains that are sticking around.
- Next, see this gold energy washing away the head trash. If the energy feels stuck, or not quite getting the area, then take the shower hose and focus the energy in this spot.
- Emotions are felt thoughts. If you notice pain in the body, there may be stuck energy in this spot. Take the hose and focus on this area.
- Notice how this energy exits out through your feet and returns to the Earth.

Lori's version

- Go into a quiet place, shut the door, and close your eyes.

- Take a few slow deep breaths and relax.
- Imagine there's a golden white light coming down from the ceiling and entering your body through the top of your head, moving down into your neck, and filling the entire trunk area of your body, then moving across your shoulders and down into your arms and hands.
- Feel your legs and feet being filled with this light.
- Your entire body is bathed in this light.
- Take another breath and relax even more.
- See this light washing over you and imagine all the negative energy, illness, discomfort, and distress leaving your body and exiting out through the soles of your feet.
- When all the stale toxic energy is gone, visualize a protective bubble filled with glorious white light surrounding your body.
- Tell yourself that for the next 24 hours, no negative energy can enter your energy fields and your body.
- Say to yourself: "I am clean, I am whole, and I am healthy."

Every time you energetically wash an item away, notice how the body feels a little lighter. Our head trash becomes a burden that weighs us down.

When Sam cleared his head trash, his appearance and attitude changed. After his healing, he looked like he'd taken 15 years off his age and he noticed that he was a lot happier.

When Lori cleared her head trash, she improved her self-image, elevated her self-esteem, and was much happier, healthier, and more relaxed.

When we work with clients on this process, they smile afterwards. Smiling is a confirmation that the garbage has been cleared. Our natural state is bliss. If you aren't happy, then there's a mental story that something is wrong. The head trash is a thief of happiness and joy.

Perform this practice for 5-10 minutes, or whatever feels right to you. Also, the shower does not need to be gold; it can be any color that feels right to you.

Here is a link for a guided meditation for a daily mental shower:

http://www.headtrashanonymous.org/media

## 12

## RECYCLING THE HEAD TRASH

The mind gets stuck in the past, telling the same old story repeatedly. These stuck thoughts are old thoughts, and nothing new comes from old thoughts. When Sam was stuck in his "woe is me" mindset, healing would have been impossible. Later he learned that a mind trapped in the past is unaware of the present moment. Lori learned that she suffered negative consequences when she wallowed in self-hatred. She noticed during the healing phase of her self-development that people responded to her according to the way she was feeling about herself. Negativity begets negativity.

*The Secret* is a book written by Rhonda Byrne on the law of attraction, which is using your thoughts to create things in your life. For example, there is an infinite abundance in the Universe. You can go to any upscale neighborhood and see wealth around you. The only thing preventing you from prosperity is your own limited mind filled with head trash.

Louise Hay said, "It's only a thought, and a thought can be changed."

Know that you're only one thought away from heaven or hell.

Changing thoughts requires you to be fully here in this moment and the mind is rarely aware of the present moment. All our power is in the present moment. Being lost in past or future thoughts is a disempowering state.

The mind is a constant stream of thoughts. You would use a mindfulness practice by placing gaps into the thought stream. By placing gaps into the thought stream, you break the habit of recycling your head trash, and you increase your inner peace. Inner peace, our natural state of Perfect Spirit, is home to lasting transformations.

Mindfulness practices are simply bringing the conscious mind to the present moment. Our conscious mind cannot dwell in thoughts and be aware of this moment. This is multi-tasking, and multi-tasking is reserved for the subconscious mind.

---

### Exercise #5: Mindfulness Practice

Pause reading the book for a moment and take 10-20 seconds to just look around at your surroundings without naming the items you see. This is a mindfulness practice.

Here are some other examples, or create your own that help bring your mind into your awareness of this moment.

1. Touch an object and notice: Hot or cold? Is the object rough or smooth? Color? Smell? Taste?

2. Place your hands under running water. Is the water hot or cold, is the flow of water fast or slow?

3. Grab an ice cube, notice the melting water.

4. Walk around your house and notice all

the details of the furniture, artwork, flooring, etc.

5. Feel your feet on the floor, and if you're walking, notice each step.

6. Pause in the present moment. When you're doing something, like walking or getting a glass of water, pause and fully notice your surroundings for 10-15 seconds. Engage all your senses in this moment without labeling or judging objects you see, since we want the mind to relax. Then continue your task.

---

This seems very simple, yet it's very effective. The mind has a story that creating transformation must be complicated. The simpler life can become, the easier life flows. A more complicated life is filled with stress and anxiety.

## 13

## NEVER CRITICIZE YOURSELF

When you criticize yourself, you're allowing your head trash to define your Perfect Spirit, which is beyond definition. Also, self-criticism creates stress, which provides the fuel for autoimmune disease. Sam had a lot of self-hate, so the body responded by attacking itself!

Stress creates a toxic inner environment, which creates disharmony in the body. This disharmony creates an energic imbalance, making the body susceptible to stress-related diseases and autoimmune diseases.

Realize that you're doing your best in this moment based on your understanding of the situation and the depth of your awareness.

The head trash fills you with regret and shame. These emotions occur when you look back at the past. When filled with regret and shame, bring yourself into the present moment, and realize where your skill level was, based on your understanding and awareness of the situation. You truly were doing your best. In each moment, we are improving our understanding of life and building our skill sets.

Remember, each experience is here for us to learn and grow from. Life is happening for your benefit. Each experience is happening at the perfect time and perfect place for our spiritual growth.

## 14

## OUR VIBRATION, OUR ENERGY

When we are born on Earth, our vibration, our energy of Perfect Spirit, is at its highest. We come directly from The Universe, Source, etc., which has the highest vibration, and we are a part of this vibration (Oneness). When we are born, we are like a bell that has been cast. The bell is flawless and has perfect pitch and tone.

Then life happens, and the head trash begins to build. Think of head trash as tape on the bell that begins to dampen our natural vibration.

When you remove each piece of head trash, you restore a piece of your vibration. In truth, we *restore* our vibration, not raise our vibration.

## 15

## THE HEAD TRASH EPIDEMIC

There is an epidemic in our world. Many people are filled with head trash, creating a "dark night of the mind." We have read that every 40 seconds, someone takes their life. We've been in this complete mental darkness. Unless you've been there, it's hard to convey this hopeless feeling into words. Regardless of the depth of head trash, it only takes one recycled negative thought to harm yourself.

The most destructive habits listed earlier all stem from the dark night of the mind—from guilt and shame, to poor self-care, to procrastination, and endless non-supportive behaviors. The head trash stories are taking you away from the truth: you are the Perfect Spirit—you are one with all that is.

We never understood the term *dark night of the soul*. The soul never goes dark. It's the mind that goes dark. In India, they use the word "namaste." Namaste means "the light within me bows to the light within you." We are an expression of the one light.

Our light is a Wayshower, our built-in guidance system. You can think of a Wayshower as a lighthouse, always pointing the way to safety, while the mind filled with head trash is trying to slam you into the rocky shores. The intuitive voice is always leading the way. We follow our intuitive voices to recover the body and mind. The mind filled with head trash is often confused and uncertain as to which path to follow. The intuitive voice comes first, and the mental voice comes second, telling you why the first voice is wrong!

## 16

## HEAD TRASH ANONYMOUS

Lori and I founded Head Trash Anonymous (trademark pending) with a mission to help individuals recover and heal from negative thought addiction. We desire a world free of head trash.

This book outlines the steps that we follow.

**Step 1** – Know yourself. Become aware of self-destructive patterns of behavior and negative thoughts. You are not your thoughts—you are Perfect Spirit.

**Step 2** – Knowing "all is well." The current experience exists to help you learn and grow. Everything is happening for your benefit.

**Step 3** – Accept, approve, and love yourself. Become empowered by noticing physical and mental positive outcomes of newly generated supportive thoughts. Don't allow the head trash to define you or destroy you.

Know that you are doing your best in this moment, based on your current understanding of the situation and the depth of your awareness.

**Step 4** – Take a daily mental shower. Take a daily inventory of how the head trash has led you away from Perfect Spirit.

**Step 5** – Freedom. When the mind is quiet, you are not filled with stress. You realize your limitless potential without head trash creating false limitations, and your intuitive voice becomes amplified.

Our goal is to have chapters throughout the world

as a life support group, a group that can remind us of the truth, since the mind often forgets.

We have chapters in New York City, Philadelphia, and a virtual chapter on Facebook – Head Trash Anonymous Global Chapter:

https://www.facebook.com/groups/1724033387906907

If you join the Facebook group, under the files is a PDF copy of Sam's first book, *I Don't Dwell*. Our gift to you.

If you are interested in creating a chapter in your community, please send an email to chapters@headtrashanonymous.org.

## 17

## OUR GREATEST ADDICTION

Our greatest addiction is our addiction to thoughts.

Sam nearly killed himself from taking his destructive thoughts as his truth. A negative thought, belief, opinion, or judgment is never true. He tended to recycle his head trash, and by repeating things over and over, he unknowingly developed habits that made life extremely difficult. By breaking the habit of negative thought addiction, he regained his health and lived a life without worry and fear.

Lori despised herself so much that she wanted to die. She obsessed constantly on escaping from a life of pain, guilt, and shame. She was addicted to her destructive, dangerous thoughts. She broke the addiction to suicidal thoughts by beginning a healing process whereby she stopped seeing a distorted view of herself and developed self-acceptance.

To break the addiction, you don't need any special tools or training, you just begin where you are. You simply need to practice, and there is no perfect practice. Perfection is judgment, a form of head trash. Perfectionism is a poison that creates procrastination. If you're hesitating about taking action to get your power back, then take a leap of faith in you!

Sam and Lori began by just sitting quietly for a few minutes a day–where will you begin? Remember, there is no prescribed formula, just your way.

CONCLUSION

Sam wasn't focused on healing; this would have been too big of a leap for his mind to accept. Sam was extremely stressed, and he simply wanted inner peace. Through inner peace, he was able to transform his life. Sam discovered the great myth that he took as his truth: "Once you lose your health, it's gone forever." Sam is living proof that miracles can and do happen. When Sam looks back at his life, it seems so surreal that he endured all that suffering.

Lori's progress was slow for many years until she took that leap into a new consciousness through daily mental relaxation. She was able to reinvent herself and change her life in a profound way. She went from a high school dropout to a college professor; from an abused woman to a strong, proud, and independent person.

When you no longer allow the mind to steal your peace and happiness, then inner peace is what remains. When inner peace is in place, you can hear your intuitive insights on the way forward for you—your unique journey.

You are the one that creates transformation. You are the keeper of your consciousness—Perfect Spirit.

We would enjoy hearing about your successes. Please send your miracle stories to miracles@headtrashanonymous.org.

All is well.

# ABOUT THE AUTHORS

### Sam Shelley, The Miracle Man

After his restored health, Sam walked away from a 20+ year IT career with no plan, just a knowing that he had a greater calling. He then became an ordained interfaith minister. He helps individuals clear their head trash and does a live Facebook show with Lori, *Soul Messages with Lori and Sam*, which provides the viewers with intuitive messages. His guilty pleasure is watching reality shows since he enjoys studying human behavior.

### Lori Pantazis

In addition to being an astrologer, healer, and counselor, Lori is a professor at a SUNY college in NYC. Lori takes daily morning yoga classes to relax, breathe, and focus. She also loves to speed walk long distances in NYC to promote her cardiovascular health. Her vision—and Sam's—is to help as many people as she can by using the Internet as a form of outreach and all-inclusiveness.

## Divine Synchronicity

Destiny, or synchronicity, was at play when I connected with Sam. A mutual friend of ours lives in Astoria, New York, and she told me about Sam's desire to eventually relocate from Pennsylvania to New York. She mentioned that he would like to live in Astoria and she asked me if I would be open to a male roommate. She also mentioned that he wanted a business partner who had similar or complementary spiritual abilities. At the time, I was experiencing financial difficulty, and I was open to the idea of having a roommate to ease my financial strife. I was also looking for a business partner; I'd previously had a potential partner who unfortunately started having health issues, and thus, the partnership never manifested. As soon as I had my first conversation with Sam, I knew this opportunity was exactly what I was trying to create. This was an ideal match. We met a few weeks later and confirmed that our beliefs were in sync. Then four days after our first meeting, Sam's mother suddenly passed away, which turned out to be the same day that my partner of 20+ years had passed away two years prior. We felt this was divine synchronicity in action, and a confirmation that we were meant to do business together.

Sam and I share the same vision to help as many people as we can to free themselves from head trash with chapters throughout the world. Our goal is to create a major shift in consciousness by helping individuals break the habit of negative thought addiction. We would also like to have a healing center and provide many services to those who want to be a part of our awesome mission and vision.

## SPECIAL THANKS

Kristen Forbes at Deviance Press for editing, interior design, and releasing this book into the world.

Marcella Dominguez, Esq for her trademark work on Head Trash Anonymous.

DesignArt for the beautiful general book cover.

Poppet 3 for the magical special edition live event book cover.

James Altucher for his book challenge that started this version of this book.

First Center Spiritual Living – NYC. We both work here part-time, and Sam has taught the Thursday night self-empowerment classes on several occasions.

Rev. Dr. Greg Harte

To my special supporters that have been with Sam throughout the years:

- Michelle and Rob Thornton
- Sarah Miller
- Kristen Peek
- Christopher Whatley
- Rishi Kanjan
- Lalitha Setty
- Evelyn Flores
- Connie Bell-Dixon
- Carol Ruth Dickerson
- Laurie McSwiggin
- Allison Twiss-O'Neil
- All the members of Head Trash Anonymous around the world

Made in the USA
Middletown, DE
01 May 2019